Purrfect

AaaaA

When
you're
smitten by
a kitten, what's
your option?
One
adoption!

Liz Brownlee

Other fantastic poetry collections from Scholastic:

Animal Poems
Dinosaur Poems
Disgusting Poems
Family Poems
Funny Poems
Magic Poems
School Poems
Silly Poems
Spooky Poems

PET POEMS

Compiled by Jennifer Curry
Illustrated by Woody Fox

SCHOLASTIC

*This book is for EMMA HATTERSLEY,
a very special girl.*

Published by Scholastic Ltd,
Book End, Range Road, Witney,
Oxfordshire OX29 0YD
www.scholastic.co.uk
Designed using Adobe InDesign

Compiled by Jennifer Curry
Internal illustrations by Woody Fox
Cover illustration by Tony De Saulles

Printed in Great Britain by CPI Group (UK) Ltd, Croydon, CR0 4YY
© 2015 Scholastic Ltd
1 2 3 4 5 6 7 8 9 5 6 7 8 9 0 1 2 3 4

British Library Cataloguing-in-Publication Data
A catalogue record for this book is available from the British Library.

ISBN 978-1407-15887-7

CONTENTS

A SHAGGY ONE WOULD DO

GLOOMSDAY, DOOMSDAY

TURKEYS JUS WANNA PLAY REGGAE

VET REQUIRED: APPLY WITHIN

MY FISH CAN RIDE A BICYCLE

WHISKERS LIKE SPIKY ICICLES

MEMORY CAT

WHAT SHALL WE CALL HIM?

A PYTHON IN THE PANTRY

LAST WORD

FIRST WORD

Pet Shop Rap

We've got a pet shop,
A noisy pet shop,
A chirping, barking pet shop,
We've got a pet shop,
A lively pet shop,
A splashing, dashing pet shop.

We've got …
Tiny gerbils
Purring cats
Cute little puppies
Black and white rats
Birds that sing
Mice that squeak
Hairy black spiders
Parrots that speak.

We've got a pet shop,
A noisy pet shop,
A chirping, barking pet shop,
We've got a pet shop,
A lively pet shop,
A splashing, dashing pet shop.

We've got …
Swimming turtles
Darting fish
Guinea pigs
Sitting in their dish
Hamsters that nibble
Snakes that glide
Rabbits that bounce
Lizards that hide.

We've got a pet shop,
A noisy pet shop,
A chirping, barking pet shop,
We've got a pet shop,
A lively pet shop,
A splashing, dashing pet shop.

Coral Rumble

HAIKU

When lessons get dull
Leave the classroom behind and
Head for Pets Corner

Jennifer Curry

COOL SCHOOL PETS

Miss Flynn's Pangolin

Miss Flynn's pangolin
Hates school dinner
And Miss Flynn's pangolin
Is growing thinner!
Miss Flynn's pangolin
Can't cope with stew
But he's mad about ants
(Which you don't have to chew)
So if Miss Flynn's pangolin
Becomes distressed
Send Miss Flynn to find him
A nice ants' nest!

Sue Cowling

Who Was Supposed to Feed the Hamster?

"Well, you see, Miss,
It was like this, Miss.
  I'm not talking to Chloe
  And Chloe's not talking to Jill
  And Jill's not talking to Zoe
  And Zoe's not talking to Will
  And Will's not talking to Harry
  And Harry's not talking to Tim
  And Tim's not talking to Larry
  And Larry's not talking to Jim
  And Jim's not talking to Amy
  And Amy's not talking to Rick
  And Rick's not talking to Maimie
  And Maimie's not talking to Flick
  And Flick's not talking to Molly
  And Molly's not talking to Dee
  And Dee's not talking Holly
  And Holly's not talking to ME.
SO – nobody
Told anybody
That somebody
Had to feed
The hamster
Today.
  Sorry!"

Jenni Sinclair

from... Me MembaWen

Me memba wen we use to be ena 4H club a
  school
We use to get bees, pigs, rabbit, fowl, goat,
An all dem tings de fe look after,
One day, more dan all
We a look after de bees, so we tek out
Some honey fe eat,
One a dem bwoy no mek sure im
Smoke off all de bees,
Im bite de honey comb wid bees pon da
De bees bite im ina in mout
Im bawl out WOH, WOH, mi mout, mi mout
An spit out de whole a it.

Frederick Williams

Subtraction

Our French teacher keeps snails,
But we get quite suspicious
When she tells us that keeping snails
Is simply "so delicious!"

She also keeps pet frogs,
She says they're good for kissing,
But what we really want to know
Is why their legs are missing!

Coral Rumble

Teacher's Pet

The teachers in my school must think
they're working in a zoo.
Their classrooms feature many a creature.
Here are just a few:

Mr Lee has a chimpanzee.
It leaps about and wriggles.
It pulls his hair and bumps his chair
and gives us all the giggles.

Mrs Drake has a ten-foot snake
inside a case of glass.
When children shout she lets it out
to quieten down the class.

Mr Matt has a vampire bat
with teeth that smile and bite.
When it's time for sums it shows its gums
and helps us get them right!

Mrs Rider wears a spider
dangling from one ear.
It does no harm. It's meant to charm,
but fills us full of fear.

Mr Breeze keeps jumping fleas
in a jar on the window sill.
I wonder why his class all cry,
"Please sir, we can't sit still."

Mrs Swish keeps angel fish.
They help to calm us down.
Their gentle glide drifts deep inside
and smoothes away each frown.

But young Miss Sweet, so nice and neat,
has the best pet there can be.
I hope she'll get no other pet,
for neat Miss Sweet has ME!

Tony Mitton

Cool School Pets

We like grizzly bears and pythons
Alligators, sewer rats.
We like Komodo dragons
And giant vampire bats.
We like man-eating tigers
And tarantulas are nice
But what are we allowed to keep?
Gerbils, *goldfish*, *mice*.

Philip Waddell

HAIKU

Our budgerigar
Happy to feed on bird seed
Longs for mimosa.

David Whitehead

MY IGUANA LOVES BANANA

 Dog Byte

When they wish me "Nighty-night"
I look bleary-eyed and gormless –
But this is just a SHAM!
As soon as they're asleep
I'm into my RAM mode!
You've heard of Pack Dogs?
Well, I'm a HACK Dog!
I wonder what they'd do
If half the neighbourhood's
Dog owners knew
Their pets have learned to use
Their owners' computers, late at night?
(We find them useful
For storing information,
Just as humans do.)

Months ago, I opened a window of my own
For where I'd buried things,
Like bones or balls.
But now that I've become a HACKER,
It's even more exciting!
I tap into the records of other computers
And find dog-run windows
That list the whens and wheres
Of *their* buried treasures,
Soon to become my own…

"A chicken carcass in the vegetable patch"
"A tasty lamb's leg at Number 4"
"Some spare ribs under the apple tree" –
Things they've been saving for a "private gnaw",
Until I dig them up – and "relocate"…
I'm building quite a collection!
And, joy of joys, no one suspects!
I've avoided all detection,
Thanks to my technological skills.

For I'm a "New-Age" Retriever –
And the results are simply GOLDEN!

Trevor Harvey

Puppy and the Sausage

He thinks that it's fighting back
When it burns his nose;
He prances all about it
Barking, making shows.

He snaps at it, but it's too hot;
Tosses it up high,
Then stops to sniff and study it
Pawing nervously.

Now suddenly, the burning cooled,
Here comes the last attack;
He grabs it in his baby teeth
And gulps the sausage back.

Gabriel Fitzmaurice

Jocelyn, My Dragon

My dragon's name is Jocelyn,
He's something of a joke.
For Jocelyn is very tame,
He doesn't like to maul or maim.
Or breathe a fearsome fiery flame;
He's much too smart to smoke.

And when I take him to the park
The children form a queue,
And say, 'What lovely eyes of red!'
As one by one they pat his head.
And Jocelyn is so well-bred,
He only eats a few!

Colin West

My Pony

velvety nostrils
nuzzle my pockets for mints
wistfully drooling

Sue Cowling

My Pet Alligator

He crawls through the rooms
He likes to watch TV
And he almost eats everything
If he can
But if he doesn't like the food
He gets very mad
So we give him food he likes
Just to be on
The safe
side.

Thomas Bull (aged 6)

Hello! How Are You? I Am Fine!

Hello! How are you? I am fine!
is all my dog will say,
he's probably repeated it
a thousand times today.
He doesn't bark his normal bark,
he doesn't even whine,
he only drones the same Hello!
How are you? I am fine!

Hello! How are you? I am fine!
his message doesn't change,
it's gotten quite monotonous,
and just a trifle strange.
Hello! How are you? I am fine!
it makes the neighbours stare,
they're unaware that yesterday
he ate my talking bear.

Jack Prelutsky

Iguana Rap

Beside the sofa sits So-Sophia;
my iguana loves ripe bananas,
she'll rap, rap, rap on my school-skirt lap,
flick out her tongue and when she's done
she'll cruise to sleep in the deep, deep heat
from the lamp inside her tank.

Under the sofa sits So-Sophia;
my iguana hates pet gymkhanas,
she'll nap, nap, nap in the tiny gap,
crawl out with ease for a bit of cheese
then cruise to sleep in the deep, deep heat
from the lamp inside her tank.

Moira Clark

HAIKU

Sleeps, eats, plays, eats; sleeps
in my favourite chair. "Grrr!"
Sleeps, eats, plays, eats, sleeps...

Mike Johnson

A SHAGGY ONE WOULD DO

Poem Left Hopefully Lying Around Before Christmas

I do want a dog.
It could be just a small one,
A shaggy one would do,
Or a smooth one or a tall one.
It needn't even be
A go-and-fetch-my-ball one;
In fact I wouldn't mind
An any-kind-at-all one.
I just want a dog.

I don't want a cat,
It would just turn up its snoot;
I don't want a sweater,
A computer or a flute;
What I'm trying to say
Is that what would best suit
(Assuming that anyone
Cares a hoot)
Is a D-O-G.

So that's it: a dog.
I wouldn't mind a Great Dane;
Or try me with a scruffy stray:
You'll find I won't complain.
I promise I'll go walks with it –
Even in the rain.
Now in case you haven't got it clear
I'll put it very plain:
Dog, dog, dog, dog, dog.

Eric Finney

The Invisible Man's Invisible Dog

My invisible dog is not much fun.
I don't know if he's sad or glum.
I don't know if, when I pat his head,
I'm really patting his bum instead.

Brian Patten

My Cocker Spaniel (Bonnie)

I'm admired for my ears. Three cheers.
I'm admired for my paws. Applause.
And if somebody chased the cat,
And if somebody chewed the mat,
And if somebody jumped the wall,
And punctured next-door neighbour's ball,
It wasn't me.

I'm admired for my eyes, surprise.
I'm admired for my smile, worthwhile.
And if somebody went upstairs,
And covered beds in doggy hairs,
And if somebody climbed a seat,
And left the marks of muddy feet,
It wasn't me.

Joanne Brown (aged 12)

It's a Dog's Life

Mum says
Our dog's
Having an identity crisis.

Yesterday,
He went out into the garden,
Then tried to come back in
Through the cat-flap.

He jammed his head so tight,
No matter how hard
We pushed and pulled
It wouldn't budge.

In the end,
We had to call the fire brigade.

When Dad came home
He nearly had a fit,
When he saw
What they'd done to the door.

He called the dog
All sorts of names.
But when the dog jumped up
To beg for his evening walk,
Dad still took him.

It's not fair.
If I'd smashed the door,
I wouldn't have been allowed out
For at least two weeks!

John Foster

War Dog

Each morning,
before breakfast,
my dog – Chewie Louie,
a shaggy, baggy
hog of a dog,
snatches and catches
his long leathered lead,
daring me to play –
"Tug of War".

Each afternoon,
after school,
my dog – Chewie Louie,
a shaggy, baggy
log of a dog,
batters and splatters me
against the front door,
glaring at me to play –
"Thug of War".

And each evening,
before bed,
my dog – Chewie Louie,
a shaggy, baggy
snog of a dog,
licks and flicks my face
with slobbering tongues of happiness,
declaring, that this time,
he wants to be friends and play –
"Hug of War"!

Ian Souter

Taking the (Shush)
For a (Shush)

He understands every word we say,
so we have to be careful.

Shall we take you-know-who
down to the green space with railings round,
to exercise his legs?
I'll find his length of leather
with the clip on the end,
and you fetch his ball –

OH! NO!
What have I said!
DOWN, BOY! DOWN!

Daphne Phillips

All the Dogs

You should have seen him –
he stood in the park and whistled,
underneath an oak tree,
and all the dogs came bounding up
and sat around him,
keeping their big eyes on him,
tails going like pendulums.
And there was one cocker pup
who went and licked his hand,
and a Labrador who whimpered
till the rest joined in.

Then he whistled a second time,
high-pitched as a stoat,
over all the shouted dog names
and whistles of owners,
till a flurry of paws
brought more dogs, panting,
as if they'd come miles,
and these too found space
on the flattened grass
to stare at the boy's
unmemorable face
which all the dogs found special.

Matthew Sweeney

My Dog, He Is an Ugly Dog

My dog, he is an ugly dog,
he's put together wrong,
his legs are much too short for him,
his ears are much too long.
My dog, he is a scruffy dog,
he's missing clumps of hair,
his face is quite ridiculous,
his tail is scarcely there.

My dog, he is a dingy dog,
his fur is full of fleas,
he sometimes smells like dirty socks,
he sometimes smells like cheese.
My dog, he is a noisy dog,
he's hardly ever still,
he barks at almost anything,
his voice is loud and shrill.

My dog, he is a stupid dog,
his mind is slow and thick,
he's never learned to catch a ball,
he cannot fetch a stick.
My dog, he is a greedy dog,
he eats enough for three,
his belly bulges to the ground,
he is the dog for me.

Jack Prelutsky

HAIKU

Behind the cupboard?
Under the stair? We've searched for
that mouse ev'rywhere.

Ann Bonner

GLOOMSDAY, DOOMSDAY

MISSING

HAVE YOU SEEN THIS MOUSE?

Last seen in the living room

Substantial reward for information!

Who's Seen Jip?

Jip's run away,
left home for good.
I just knew he would,
for earlier today
he was shouted at by dad.
"Bad dog!
Bad dog!
BAD!"

Now Jip's a stray.
What will he eat?
Where will he sleep?
I'm so sad I could weep.
Oh, gloomsday, doomsday,
my dog has gone.

Who's seen Jip?

Anyone?

Wes Magee

Missing Persons

The world's most enigmatic smile
Belongs to Crunch, our crocodile,
Who likes to lie in silent wait
Beside our shrubby garden gate.

And so detectives sometimes come
To question me and Dad and Mum
About the people, big and small,
Who seem to vanish when they call.

But nothing comes of it, of course,
Although we suffer some remorse,
For as they seek a sign or clue
Detectives seem to vanish too.

Colin Thiele

Bad Design

A hedgehog misses
children's kisses
their cuddles, coddles, tickles.
Rabbits or mice
seem twice as nice
designed without the prickles.

A nasty, porcupiney skin
will not allow a tickle in –
so tickles, kisses, cuddles, coddles
go to all the furry models.

Jez Alborough

Pet Palindrome

A palindrome is a word or a group of words that reads the same forwards and backwards. Can you find the palindrome in the following rhyme?

You can step on a carpet,
A rug or a mat,
And there'll be
Little cause for regrets;
But just mind the tortoise
The dog and the cat.
I'm telling you:
Step on no pets!

Eric Finney

Marmalade

He's buried in the bushes,
with dock leaves round his grave,
A crimecat desperado
and his name was Marmalade.
He's the cat that caught the pigeon,
that stole the neighbour's meat...
and tore the velvet curtains
and stained the satin seat.
He's the cat that spoilt the laundry,
he's the cat that spilt the stew,
and chased the lady's poodle
and scratched her daughter too.

But –
No more we'll hear his cat-flap,
or scratches at the door,
or see him at the window,
or hear his catnap snore.
So –
Ring his grave with pebbles,
erect a noble sign –
For here lies Mr Marmalade
and Marmalade was MINE.

Peter Dixon

The Great Gerbil Hunt

I've looked on the table,
I've searched through the fridge;
the cheese box is empty
I've felt in each vase!
I've checked under carpets,
beneath the settee,
behind every cushion,
below the TV...

Yes, I'm sure that I closed it,
honestly Dad –
I knew if I didn't
you'd really be mad!
Yes, I know he was safe
when I last saw him, Mum...
Well, I think that I'm sure...
Yes, I'm sure that I am!

That is...
I'm sure he'll soon come...

LOOK OUT!
DON'T STEP BACK, MUM!

Judith Nicholls

HAIKU

Peter parrot pecks,
picks on my poorly pinkie –
I'll tweak his keen beak

Moira Clark

TURKEYS JUS WANNA PLAY REGGAE

Dad's Pigeon

Now pigeon-racing is a sport
That dad was keen on trying.
Alas, the bird that daddy bought
Was terrified of flying.

'Well, who's a pretty pigeon then?'
Said daddy, as he threw it.
The pigeon fell to earth again;
'You twit!' cried dad. 'You blew it!'

'You've got to flap you wings,' said dad.
'Now practise, get acquainted!'
The pigeon flapped its wings like mad,
Took off, then promptly fainted.

To help the pigeon understand
Dad gave a demonstration,
He flapped, he jumped and came to land
In mother's rose plantation.

My dad is slowly on the mend,
My mother's still in shock,
And me? I take our feathered friend
For walkies round the block.

Doug Macleod

Quack, Quack!

We have two ducks. One blue. One black.
And when our blue duck goes "Quack-quack"
our black duck quickly quack-quacks back.
The quacks Blue quacks make her quite a
  quacker
but Black is a quicker quacker-backer.

Dr Seuss

Talking Turkeys!

Be nice to yu turkeys dis christmas
Cos turkeys just wanna hav fun
Turkeys are cool, turkeys are wicked
An every turkey has a Mum.
Be nice to yu turkeys dis christmas,
Don't eat it, keep it alive,
I could be yu mate an not on yu plate
Say, Yo! Turkey I'm on your side.

I got lots of friends who are turkeys
An all of dem fear christmas time,
Dey wanna enjoy it, dey say humans destroyed it
An humans are out of dere mind,
Yeah, I got lots of friends who are turkeys
Dey all have a right to a life,
Not to be caged up an genetically made up
By any farmer an his wife.

Turkeys jus wanna play reggae
Turkey's jus wanna hip-hop
Can yu imagine a nice young turkey saying,
"I cannot wait for de chop"?
Turkeys like getting presents, dey wanna watch
    christmas TV,
Turkeys hav brains an turkeys feel pain
In many ways like yu an me.

I once knew a turkey called
Turkey
He said, "Benji explain to me please,
Who put de turkey in christmas
An what happens to christmas trees?"
I said, "I am not too sure turkey
But it's nothing to do wid Christ Mass
Humans get greedy an waste more dan need be
An business men mek loadsa cash."

Be nice to yu turkey dis christmas
Invite dem indoors fe sum greens
Let dem eat cake an let dem partake
In a plate of organic grown beans,
Be nice to yu turkey dis christmas
An spare dem de cut of de knife,
Join Turkeys United an dey'll be delighted
An yu will mek new friends "FOR LIFE".

Benjamin Zephaniah

My Parakeet

I'm in love with my parakeet
From his beak down to his feet
Every time I hear him tweet
Hearts a-flutter, wings a-beat

Words I say he will repeat
As you all can see
I'm in love with my parakeet
And he's in love with me

Paul Cookson

Barry's Budgie! Beware!

Dave's got a dog the size of a lion
Half-wolf, half-mad, frothing with venom
It chews up policemen and then spits them out
But it's nowt to the bird I'm talking about.

Claire's got a cat as wild as a cheetah
Scratching and hissing, draws blood by the litre
Jumps high walls and hedges, fights wolves on
   its own
But there's one tough budgie it leaves well
   alone.

Murray my eel has teeth like a shark
Don't mess with Murray, he'll zap out a spark
But when Barry's budgie flies over the houses
Murray dips down his lights, blows his own fuses.

This budgie's fierce, a scar down its cheek
Tattoos on its wings, a knife in its beak
Squawks wicked words does things scarcely legal
Someone should tell Barry it's really an eagle.

David Harmer

Sergeant Brown's Parrot

Many policemen wear upon their shoulders
Cunning little radios. To pass away the time
They talk about the traffic to them, listen to the news,
And it helps them to Keep Down Crime

But Sergeant Brown, he wears upon his shoulder
A tall green parrot as he's walking up and down
And all the parrot says is "Who's-a-pretty-boy-then?"
"I am," says Sergeant Brown.

Kit Wright

HAIKU

Sad eyes. Twitching legs.
He looks so lost and afraid
On the vet's table.

John Kitching

At the Vet's

When we took our dog to the vet's
we sat and waited with all sorts of pets.

There were hamsters with headaches
and fish with the flu,
there were rats and bats
and a lame kangaroo.

There were porcupines
with spines that were bent
and a poodle that must have been
sprinkled with scent.

There were dogs that were feeling
terribly grumpy
and monkeys with mumps looking
awfully lumpy.

There were rabbits with rashes
and foxes with fleas,
there were thin mice in need of
a large wedge of cheese.

There were cats complaining
of painful sore throats,
there were gerbils and geese
and two travel-sick goats.

There were two chimpanzees
who both had toothache,
and the thought of the vet
made everyone **shake**!

Brian Moses

At the Vet's

You think you're top dog?
Lie down! Wait quietly! Here
all pets are equal.

Anne Allinson

Dream Pet

I dreamed I owned a dinosaur,
I kept it as a pet,
He really caused a panic
When I took him to the vet.

I shoved him in the waiting room,
A woman gave a shout,
The dogs all started barking
So I had to take him out.

The dinosaur was so afraid
He hid behind a car.
The vet said, "You're too big to hide,
I know just where you are!"

Before the vet could calm him down
He'd galloped to the park,
His big teeth made a racket
As they chattered in the dark!

Sue Benwell

Respect, Respect Your Cyberpet

I went to the vet
with my cyberpet
but he said,
"Nothing's been invented yet
to detect what makes a cyberpet
feel dejected and rejected
and start to fret –

"But I'd like to bet
that if your pet gets wet,
it will jump on board a jumbo jet
and fly to the sun
to try to forget
that though you know
you love and respect it,
your cyberpet just feels lost and neglected.

"So when you're alone at home
filled up with regret,
I'd like you to take some time and reflect
that a vet can do nothing
for a cyberpet.

"And before you're met with any more debt,
let your pet get connected
to an electronic vet –
you can download one from the Internet!"

Dave Ward

Vet Required: Apply Within

My pet is a monster,
a monster is my pet
and one day I decided
that he should see the vet.

The vet said, "What's the problem,
is he off his food?"
I said, "No, his appetite is monstrous,
mega, amazing, you'd…"

"Open wide," said the vet.

"…be shocked at what he guzzles;
cardboard, carpets, cassettes.
He eats absolutely everything,
even…oh dear…vets!"

Bernard Young

What Asana Wanted For Her Birthday

Please don't get me
a hamster or budgie.
Please don't get me
a goldfish or canary.

Please get me something
a little scary.
Maybe something
a wee bit hairy.

How about a tarantula?
What's wrong with a spider-pet?
If it gets sick of course
I'll take it to scare –
I mean; to see
– the vet.

Grace Nichols

HAIKU

Glitter, my goldfish,
Blows bubbles for me – kisses
Round and wet and sweet.

Jenni Sinclair

MY FISH CAN RIDE A BICYCLE

The Hopeful Frog

I had a frog whose name was Jim,
I was extremely fond of him.
He turned into a Prince one day,
I shook my head and ran away.

Daphne Schiller

Mary Had a Crocodile

Mary had a crocodile
That ate a child each day;
But interfering people came
And took her pet away.

Anon

My Fish Can Ride a Bicycle

My fish can ride a bicycle,
my fish can climb a tree,
my fish enjoys a glass of milk,
my fish takes naps with me.

My fish can play the clarinet,
my fish can bounce a ball,
my fish is not like other fish,
my fish can't swim at all.

Jack Prelutsky

Ode to a Goldfish

O
Wet
Pet!

Gyles Brandreth

Small Pet Poem

My newt
is
minute.

Mike Johnson

Hello!

HAIKU

Don't tell anyone
I have a ... The others
are afraid of them.

Ann Bonner

A Reasonable Rat

I know a really ravishing reason to become your perfectly plausible pet.

I'm a wriggily, wittily, well-behaved wonder

Have you guessed who I am yet?

No, you really cannot fail. And yes, that is the end of my tale...

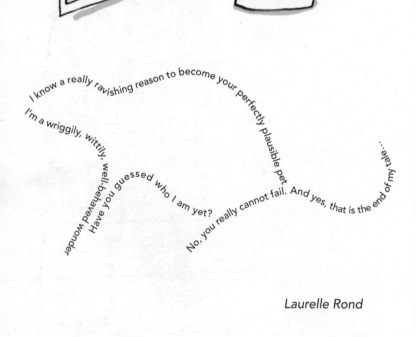

Laurelle Rond

Pocket Friends

Having your pets
close by is nice.
In this pocket
I've got two mice,
and in the other
a pink-eyed rat.
The gerbils ride
inside my hat.
I prefer things
not too big,
like this pygmy
guinea-pig…

but can you get
a kangaroo
that's big enough
to carry you?

Mark Bones

Who Am I?

My first is in guinea pig but not found in mouse.
My second's in elephant and also in louse.
My third is in rabbit. It isn't in cat.
My fourth is in budgie. You'll find it in bat.
My fifth's in iguana. It's absent from lamb.
My last is in lion, but not found in ram.

If you put first things first
You'll know who I am.
I won't need to draw you
A big diagram.

If the answer's not plain yet,
And that's what you feel,
Imagine the scene
As I race round a wheel!

John Kitching

Answer: a gerbil

Rosie Super Rabbit

Rosie my rabbit is super big.
She can run as fast as a jet
And as fast as Concorde.
Her teeth are long and yellow
  like knives.
She has two at the top and
  two at the bottom
And her whiskers are like spiky icicles.
Her ears stick up like two fingers.
They have got veins.
They are pink – like lipstick
And so are her eyes.
She has got a sniffy nose.
Her fur is as white and soft as the middle bit of bread
(except for the dirty bits on the bottom of her feet).
She crunches up dandelion leaves
And sometimes she can fly
(but don't tell anyone).
She lies down on my legs
But she scratches me sometimes.

Alex Coburn (aged 4)

My Rabbit

My rabbit
has funny habits.

When I say sit
he sits.

When he hears me call
he wags
his tail a bit.

When I throw a ball
he grabs it.

What a funny rabbit!

One day in the park
I swore I heard him bark.

John Agard

Have a Hamster!

We bought our little Hammy
An exercising wheel.
And while we watch the telly,
He just *loves* to make it squeal.

It goes round and round and round and round
And round and round and round.
Amazing how a little thing
Makes such a piercing sound.

And when he isn't wheeling
He'll be trying to eat his cage.
He'll climb up in one corner
And attack it for an age.

He goes dong-dong-dong-dong-dong-
  gong-bong
As he chews and chews and chews,
Especially when there's music on
Or some interesting news.

We love him ever such a lot
But now we've thought it through –
We think he'd be much happier
If he came to live with you.

Ian Whybrow

The Cat's Thoughts About How We Could Have Avoided Scraping Our Knuckles Trying to Get This Huge Table Through Our Kitchen Door

If only you had whiskers
Like the ones we pussies wear,
You might have turned that sideways
And there'd be no need to swear.

Ian Whybrow

HAIKU

My cat has a bell
so birds are warned she's coming.
She comes with music.

Philip Burton

MEMORY CAT

I Had a Little Cat

I had a little cat called Tim Tom Tay,
I took him to town on market day,
I combed his whiskers, I brushed his tail,
I wrote on a label, "Cat for Sale.
Knows how to deal with rats and mice.
Two pounds fifty. Bargain price."

But when the people came to buy
I saw such a look in Tim Tom's eye
That it was clear as clear could be
I couldn't sell Tim for a fortune's fee.
I was shamed and sorry, I'll tell you plain,
And I took home Tim Tom Tay again.

Charles Causley

My Cat

My cat
got fatter
and fatter.
I didn't know
what was the matter.
Then,
know what she did?
She went into the cupboard
and hid.

She was fat when she went in,
but she came out
thin.
I had a peep.
Know what I saw?
Little kittens
all in a heap –
1 – 2 – 3 – 4.

My cat's great.

Nigel Gray

Cat

My cat is black as darkest night
When no moon rides.
His eyes are green as starlit pools
And midnight tides.

But whenever the day is warm and sunny
His eyes are gold and clear as honey.
He rolls on his back and very soon
His coat is dusty with afternoon.

Ann Bonner

Animal Rights

Our cat
Won't use the cat-flap
Any more.
He's started to fight
For his Animal Rights
And insists
That he uses the door.

Lindsay MacRae

Memory Cat

I called my cat Shack-Two

Shack the First was a footballer,
Shackleton the Great.
Pride of Sunderland town.
Fleet of foot and lithe of limb.
With muscles that rippled as he ran
And hair that shone like silk.
Shack-One, my childhood hero,
The stuff of schoolgirl dreams.

But Shack-Two was my cat.
Every day, at 4 o'clock,
He'd meet me
Coming back from school,
High-stepping his way
Along the railings
That for me were shoulder-high,
And together, head-to-head,
We'd run along the street
That led to home, and milk
And toast for tea. And all the while
His blunt nose bumping at my face,
His rough tongue rasping on my cheek,
His purring noisy in my ear,
And his proud black plume of a tail
Writing exclamations of delight
In the air about me.

I loved him, my cat Shack,
When I was just a child.
I went back last year
To the street where once I lived,
And looked along the railings,
Waist-high now, remembering him.

And then he came, my memory-cat.
High-stepping his way towards me
From out of my childhood time,
Fleet of foot and lithe of limb,
With muscles that rippled as he ran
And hair that shone like silk.
And his purring was like music
In my ear.

Jenny Craig

My Lovely Pussy Cat

We have a cat her name is Lizzy
Her games make me fairly dizzy.
She licks, she purrs, she sits and begs
And plays with my mum's pegs.
When she scratches at the door
You would think she's not been fed before.
She even rides upon my swing
And doesn't seem to fear a thing.
Now she's curled up fast asleep,
Is she really counting sheep?
No, she's not. She's counting mice,
My pussy cat's life is rather nice.

Joanne Mathieson (aged 7)

HAIKU

My cat slinks, black-backed
Through the dark streets of midnight.
His name is Shadow.

Jennifer Curry

WHAT SHALL WE CALL HIM?

A Parrot Called Mouse

My Grandad has a parrot living in his house –
it talks with a squeak, so he calls it Mouse.
Its feathers flutter with a glitter of blue and gold.
It's quite cheeky even though it's quite old.
Grandad grumbles and grunts when it's time for
  bed –
he knows old Mouse has other ideas instead:
with its bold beak it shrieks as it flies free

"Can't catch
  me"

"Can't catch
  me"

"Can't catch
  me"

Tim Pointon

Our Dog Smartie

Our dog looks like a tube on legs
and he's ever so sweet
so we call him Smartie!
He's a blotchy brown and white colour
with huge ears that look like sheepskin mitts
that have been stitched to the side of his head.
And when he starts to run
they seem to be trying to clap
but never quite meet.

Unfortunately Smartie likes and loves to chew
and I mean chew, everything and anything:

carpets, curtains, shoes and doors
chairs, kitchens, gardens and floors,
newspapers, fridges, clothes and toys
bedrooms, televisions and even little boys!

And he especially enjoys legs:

Legs of beds,
legs of tables,
legs of chairs
and his favourite delicacy – legs of postmen!

But yesterday Smartie became very unsmartie!
You see Dad and I were in the attic playing
  snooker
when Dad went to pot the black.
The cue ball scorched across the green felt
and walloped into the black ball
which then slammed it into the pocket!
"Yes," shouts Dad, "I win!"
"Oh no," whispers me, "you don't!"
For the ball doesn't stop there,
it explodes out of the hole,
and flies across the room –
ZZZZZZZZZOOOOOOMMMMM –
crashing into one of Mum's newly framed
  pictures!

Guess who had gone and chewed the pockets?

But guess who Mum chewed up later!

Ian Souter

Four Crazy Pets

I've four crazy pets, all rather jolly –
Rover, Tiddles, Flopsy and Polly.
A dog, a rabbit, a parrot and a cat.
Which one's which? Can you guess that?

Rover's a dog? No!
Tiddles is a cat? No!
Flopsy's a rabbit? No!
Polly's a parrot? No!

My dog has the appetite of a small gorilla.
We called her Polly 'cause we can never fill her.

The rabbit has a habit of wetting where
  we're standing.
We call him Tiddles 'cause the puddles
  keep expanding.

Our cat purrs like an engine turning over
Vroom vroom vroom – so we call her Rover.

The fact that our parrot cannot fly is such
  a shame.
Flopsy by nature and Flopsy by name.

Four crazy names! Wouldn't you agree?
I think my pets fit their names purrfectly.

Paul Cookson

What Shall We Call the Dog?

What shall we call our new dog?
He's got to have a name.
Roger? Rover? Rufus? Rex?
No, all of those sound tame.
What shall we call him then?
Come on, it's got to sound just right.
Marcus? Martin? Marlow? Max?
No, none of those fits him quite.
For days the question still remained:
What shall we call the dog?
Tanga? Thomas? Tarquin? Terry?
Taurus? Tarzan? Trog?
No, those won't do. What shall it be?
Benedict? Brown? Brunel?
No, we simply call him Whatshall –
And he likes it very well.

Eric Finney

Cat

My cat has got no name,
We simply call him Cat;
He doesn't seem to blame
Anyone for that.

For he is not like us
Who often, I'm afraid,
Kick up quite a fuss
If *our* names are mislaid.

As if, without a name,
We'd be no longer there
But like a tiny flame
Vanish in bright air.

My pet, he doesn't care
About such things as that:
Black buzz and golden stare
Require no name but Cat.

Vernon Scannel

HAIKU

Can you believe it?
An *elephant* for Christmas!
Dad must be joking!

John Kitching

A PYTHON IN THE PANTRY

Wild Thing

I caught
a caterpillar
Kept it in a jar
to be my pet.

But I had to let it go
soaring to the sky,
too beautiful by far
to keep, when it
became a butterfly.

Ann Bonner

Our Hippopotamus

We thought a lively pet to keep
Might be a hippopotamus.
Now see him sitting in a heap,
And notice at the bottom – us.

Colin West

Ernie – the Great Collector

"Exotic Ernie" keeps the oddest creatures,
Anything that's wriggly, scaly, slick.
The neighbours think he's dangerous and dotty
But collecting reptiles gives him a real kick.

There's a salamander snoozing in the cellar
A python in the pantry he calls Pru
Tadpoles in the teapot
Two toads in the bread tin
And a lizard licking
Limescale from the loo.

One lump or two?

There's a slow worm sucking "Mintoes" on the sofa
And eight iguanas on the garage wall
A tortoise on the telly
And a dead frog in the fridge
Who's waiting till
The undertaker calls.

Now Mrs Ernie says she's going to leave him,
She says she needs more space in which to spread.
"You always were a fusspot," Ernie mutters.
"I like an alligator in the bed."

Patricia Leighton

My Stick Insect Is Hiding

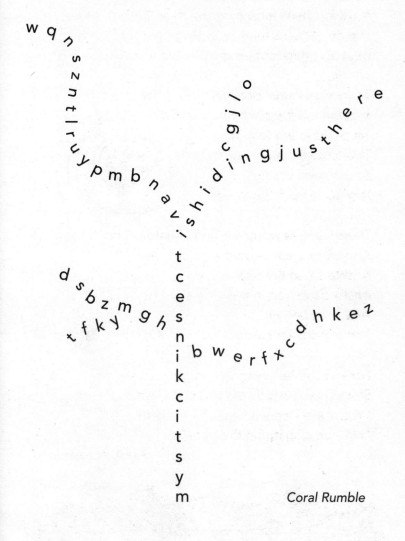

Coral Rumble

A Perfect Pet

Now you have a papagouli
do be sure to treat it right –
he's a rather tender creature
and he doesn't like the light.

If you take him out in sunshine
that purple fur will fade,
and his tail will lose its curl
if you keep him in the shade.

He really can't see anything
unless the place is dark,
and if he doesn't see you
he will scrunch you like a shark.

Be sure he wears dark glasses
when you have to hit the trail –
take a really big umbrella
with an opening for his tail.

If he sneezes he gets savage,
ninety-nine things make him sneeze
and he's equally bad-tempered
if he's ruffled by the breeze.

A most demanding creature,
quite a problem, you can see –
now you have a papagouli
and my deepest sympathy.

Barbara Giles

Luv Song

I am in luv wid a hedgehog
I've never felt dis way before
I have luv fe dis hedgehog
And everyday I luv her more an more,
She lives by de shed
Where weeds an roses bed
An I just want de world to know
She makes me glow.

I am in luv wid a hedgehog
She's making me hair stand on edge,
So in luv wid dis hedgehog
An her friends
Who all live in de hedge
She visits me late
An eats off Danny's plate
But Danny's a cool tabby cat
He leaves it at dat.

I am in luv wid a hedgehog
She's gone away so I must wait
But I do miss my hedgehog
Everytime she goes to hibernate.

Benjamin Zephaniah

Pink Pet

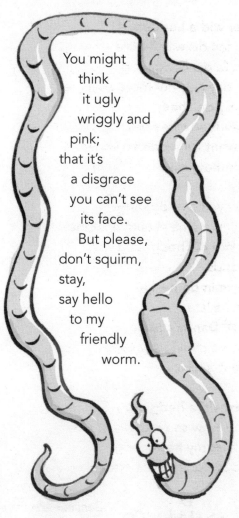

You might
think
it ugly
wriggly and
pink;
that it's
a disgrace
you can't see
its face.
But please,
don't squirm,
stay,
say hello
to my
friendly
worm.

Tim Pointon

The Yak

As a friend to the children commend me the Yak.
You will find it exactly the thing:
It will carry and fetch, you can ride on its back,
Or lead it about with a string.

The Tartar who dwells on the plains of Tibet
(A desolate region of snow)
Has for centuries made it a nursery pet,
And surely the Tartar should know!

Then tell your papa where the Yak can be got,
And if he is awfully rich
He will buy you the creature – or else he will not.
(I cannot be positive which.)

Hilaire Belloc

My Pet Mouse

I have a friendly little mouse,
He is my special pet.
I keep him safely on a lead.
I haven't lost him yet.

I never need to feed him,
Not even bits of cheese.
He's never chased by any cat
And he does just as I please.

He likes it when I stroke him
for he's smooth and grey and fat.
He helps me sometimes with my games,
When he runs around my mat.

I've never ever known a mouse
That could really be much cuter.
He's my extra special 'lectric mouse
That works my home computer.

David Whitehead

The Thing About Aardvarks

If you put them in a football team
they wouldn't score a goal
If you took them to a golf course
they'd never find the hole
If they're boxing with a squirrel
they'll come back badly beaten
They cannot win Monopoly
even if they're cheating
If someone let a stink-bomb off
they'd be the last to smell it
If you ask them to write down their name
they'll ask you how to spell it.

And even in the 'egg & spoon'
they're bringing up the rear
They never break the finishing tape
to hear a thunderous cheer
And yet there is place
where they are sure of victory
For the aardvark always comes first
in the English dictionary.

Lindsay MacRae

Auntie Babs

Auntie Babs became besotted
With her snake, so nicely spotted,
Unaware that pets so mottled
Like to leave their keepers throttled.

Colin West

LAST WORD

A Pet Is...

A pet is a creature
with nothing to do,
its food and shelter
provided by you.

It might be a cat
(with a life of its own)
or a dog, or a horse
(less happy alone).

Or maybe a goldfish,
stick insect, white mouse,
a bird or a snake
has its home in your house.

It really depends
on the time and the space
you can devote
to your pet, in your place.

A tiger or hippo,
a whale or raccoon
are less likely lodgers
in any spare room.

A pet is a creature
with nothing to do
since its life and its living
depend on – just you.

Jane Whittle

Acknowledgements

The publishers gratefully acknowledge permission to reproduce the following copyright material:

Jez Alborough for the use of 'Bad Design'.

Sue Benwell for the use of 'Dream Pet'.

Mark Bones for the use of 'Pocket Friends'.

Gyles Brandreth for the use of 'Ode to a Goldfish'.

Liz Brownlee for the use of 'Purrfect'.

Philip Burton for the use of 'My Cat Has a Bell'.

Caroline Sheldon Literary Agency for the use of 'My Rabbit' from *Another Day on Your Foot and I Would Have Died* by John Agard. © 1983, John Agard (1983, Macmillan Children's Books).

Paul Cookson for the use of 'Four Crazy Pets' from *Sing That Joke* by Paul Cookson. © 1998, Paul Cookson (1998, Paternoster Publishing) and 'My Parakeet'.

Sue Cowling for the use of 'My Pony' and 'Miss Flynn's Pangolin'.

Jennifer Curry for the use of 'Who Was Supposed to Feed the Hamster?' and 'Glitter My Goldfish' by Jenni Sinclair, and 'Memory Cat' by Jenny Craig.

Curtis Brown Group Ltd, London for the use of 'What Asana Wanted for Her Birthday' from *Asana and the Animals* by Grace Nichols. © 1997, Grace Nichols (1997, Walker Books).

David Higham Associates for the use of 'Teachers Pet' by Tony Mitton from *Teachers Pets* by Paul Cookson, © 1999, Tony Mitton (1999, Macmillan) and 'I Had a Little Cat' from *Collected Poems for Children* by Charles Causley, © 1996, Charles Causley (1996, Macmillan).

Trevor Dickinson for the use of 'Sad Eyes', 'Who Am I?' and 'Can You Believe It?'.

Peter Dixon for the use of 'Marmalade' from *Grow Your Own Poems* by Peter Dixon. © 1988, Peter Dixon (1988, Macmillan Education).

Sheilagh Finney for the use of 'Poem Left Hopefully Around Before Christmas', 'Pet Palindrome' and 'What Shall We Call the Dog?' by Eric Finney.

Daphne Phillips for the use of 'Taking the (Shush) for a (Shush)'.

Rogers, Coleridge and White for the use of 'The Invisible Man's Invisible Dog' from *Thawing Frozen Frogs* by Brian Patten. © 2012, Brian Patten (2012, Frances Lincoln Children's Books).

Laurelle Rond for the use of 'A Reasonable Rat'.

Coral Rumble for the use of 'My Stick Insect Is Hiding', 'Pet Shop Rap' and 'Subtraction'.

Daphne Schiller for the use of 'The Hopeful Frog'.

The Peters Fraser and Dunlop Group for the use of 'The Yak' from *Cautionary Tales* by Hilaire Belloc. © 1993, Hilare Belloc (1993, Random House).

United Agents for the use of 'Have a Hamster' and 'The Cat's Thoughts About How We Could Have Avoided Scraping Our Knuckles Trying to Get This Huge Table Through Our Kitchen Door' by Ian Whybrow.

Philip Waddell for the use of 'Cool School Pets'.

Dave Ward for the use of 'Respect, Respect, Your Cyberpet'.

Colin West for the use of 'Jocelyn My Dragon', 'Our Hippopotamus' and 'Auntie Babs'.

David Whitehead for the use of 'Our Budgerigar' and 'My Pet Mouse'.

Jane Whittle for the use of 'A Pet Is...'.

Kit Wright for the use of 'Sergeant Brown's Parrot' from *Rabbiting On* by Kit Wright. © 1986, Kit Wright (1986, HarperCollins).

Bernard Young for the use of 'Vet Required: Apply Within' from *Brilliant!* by Bernard Young. © 2000, Bernard Young (2000, Kingston Press).

Every effort has been made to trace copyright holders for the works reproduced in this book, and the publishers apologise for any inadvertent omissions.